ME,
MYSELF,
AND
I...AM

MARQ
POWELL

Beloved, I wish above all things that thou mayest prosper and be in health, even as thy soul prospereth.

3 John 1:2 KJV

ME, MYSELF, & I...AM

ISBN: 9781793037121

Cover design: Christie Wade

DEDICATIONS

All the honor and all the glory belong to God. He literally trusted me to be a steward of the gifts He placed in my DNA to be used as one of many tools on this earth for the building of His kingdom. God thank you, for believing in me, especially when I didn't believe in myself.

To my son Daniel. I hope the things I have done and the life I live has set some form of example you can follow that will help you become the great man God has destined you to be.

To Howard, my stepfather. Man, you have been nothing less than a father to me. You have always treated me and loved me like your own flesh and blood. My love and respect for you is beyond measure.

To Rose, my stepmother. You have always looked out for me. You have a special gift of caring for anyone that needs help. I'm one of those people.

To all my family and friends who have supported me throughout my life and ministry. Thank you.

SPECIAL DEDICATION TO MY PARENTS

James Powell and Catherine Brown

Dad, as I have matured in ministry, I've come to value the intelligence and wisdom you possess. You've shown me when you hear God's voice and He has given you an assignment, then just trust Him and DO IT. Like Noah, a voice called you, faith led you, and stubbornness pushed you to build an ark of safety. You worked alone while some laughed, and others wondered. Every time I walk into that church, it reminds me of your faith. On the natural side, your stubbornness can be a little annoying, but on the spiritual side it is one of God's greatest weapons against Satan and the greatest asset for building the kingdom of God. Some see you as traditional, but I have seen you as a trendsetter. No matter how much I think I know, you always show me there is more. You have shown me what true ministry is.

Mom, you have exemplified the true essence of love, sacrifice, and strength. You are truly the model of a mother that anyone would be blessed to have. You made sure I had every opportunity to pursue my dreams. You encouraged me and tried to make sure every resource I needed was at my disposal.

Thank you both for what you have instilled in me to be who I am today. I love you both.

TO MY WIFE DORIS

Wow, I don't know where to start. You have been with me longer than anyone. We practically raised each other. You have always tried to pull the best out of me. There is no question that you have been the rock I have leaned on through these years.

When all was good we celebrated. When things went bad you stayed and fought with me. When I was wounded, you nurtured me. When I made bad decisions, you forgave me.

You always make it clear that whatever you have is mine as well. You have more than proven that over and over.

You have blessed me in more ways than you can imagine. Your sense of humor, your compassion for others, your giving heart are all gifts of God. To think that God gave that whole wonderful package to me.

You have been there through all the ups and downs. You have supported every dream I have chased. God knew exactly what He was doing when He gave me you.

Thank you so much for imparting into me. I can't help but love you and spoil you.

Contents

INTRODUCTION

Galatians 5:16 tells us to walk in the spirit and we won't fulfil the lust of the flesh. There are three words in this verse that display a strong sense of significance that need to be examined to further understand the aptness of this passage. The three words are spirit, lust, and flesh. There is also a fourth word that is implied, and that is the word soul. This will be discussed later.

To begin the breakdown of what Paul was saying, we must go back to the beginning of man. In Genesis 2:7, *"And the Lord God formed man of the dust of the ground, and breathed into his nostrils the breath of life; and man became a living soul."*

Just as there are three attributes of God: Father (supremacy of God), Son (word of God), and Holy Ghost (breath of God). Man is also made of three entities. Man is a spirit living in a body focused through a soul. How did this come to be?

In the days of God creating the heavens, the earth, and all therein, He spoke everything into existence by simply saying "Let there be". But when it came to Him creating man, He did something different. It was a prominent exhibition of what would become the beginning of the greatest love story of all time. The story of a creator who loves with a love of no conditions and intensively seeks for a freewill return of that same love from His very own creation that He would call man.

Man would be given the keys and full authorization over all creation accept one tree. He didn't need to be covered with cloths or skins but would be draped with God's glory. The love God displayed for man and the reverence man felt for God were both unequivocal. But this unadulterated relationship of impeccable love would soon be challenged with a single persuasion implanted in man's mind by an evil force that would cause a perpetual rift between the two.

When man's noncompliance to Gods dictation to not eat of the tree of the knowledge of good and evil happened, sin burst through the doors of disobedience, and like a belligerent infestation profaned the arrant purpose of God.

God had to implement a plan that would restore man back to his former glory and repair the relationship that has now been tainted. Through a series of events God has been making an appeal to man to return to Him and that regardless of what he has done He forgives him. But at the same time Satan has a counter plan to hinder this repair through subtle deceits.

Satan knows that for him to have a chance at succeeding with his agenda, he had to study and understand the composite of man. On the other hand, for us to develop a defense and execute the perfect offense, we must first know who we are ourselves because the enemy has already acquired that information.

We usually refer to the entities of ourselves as Me, Myself, and I, but because we have the spirit of God in us, we have a fourth component. That fourth part is the I AM of God. When Moses asked God, who would he say sent him, God responded, "I Am That I Am". Which simply means, He is.

1 John 4:4 tells us that the God that is in us is greater than anyone that's in the world. This means we can do all things through Christ, who is the word of God, who strengthens us, Philippians 4:13. Everything we need is in God and because "HE IS", then that means, "WE ARE". Whatever we need God to be is what God wants us to be.

Satan doesn't want us to fully comprehend this revelation. Through trickery, deceit, and distractions, he constantly scrambles the access code to the arsenal of unlimited authority we have in God that can destroy him.

The main deception he implants in our minds is that we are alone in this battle or will make us feel that God's love is predicated on our actions and not being the righteousness of God.

Children of God, you must realize that the devil is powerful but has no power. He is only as strong as you allow him to be. You have authority over him, not vice-versa. If you resist, he must run from you. Stop saying you beat him running or you and he were in a fight and you got away. He must submit to your commands because God has given you the authority.

Hopefully this book will help you understand who you are, what you are, and whose you are, that you are not alone, and you are the righteousness of God. You will learn how the THAT of God is what ties us together with Him. You will see how you are composed of Me, Myself and I...AM.

You will also come to understand how the enemy can infiltrate our being and continues to try deterring our full restoration to God and our happiness on earth.

Chapter 1: *The Body*

"ME"

The state of existence; Being

Me is the state of being, which is the overall physical condition of a person, as opposed to someone's state of mind. It is the existence of a thing. Man didn't exist until God created him. You didn't exist until your father's seed fertilized your mother's egg, then you came into existence. Or shall I say...You came to be.

The word flesh in the opening scripture in the Greek is sarx, which means human nature or the body.

Imagine God speaking from His powerful throne into the essence of nothingness, the things He wanted to become... and they simply became. But when He decided to make man, He stepped off His throne and stood on the soil of the earth. He stomped His foot on the ground and dust arose. He gathered the dust particles together and formed a body. This conception of such precision, detail, craftiness, and even a touch of poignancy was created, not with His words but with His own loving hands. This body was just that... a body. It had no life, no love, and no thought. It was an empty house with no occupant.

God made the human with mechanical and scientific exactness. Let's look at some of the captivating elements of this organic architectural marvel.

The human skeleton is composed of 270 bones at birth, but it decreases to 206 by adulthood after some bones have fused together. There are over 650 named skeletal muscles, 360 joints, over 7 trillion nerve endings, approximately 1,320 tendons, 900 ligaments, 78 organs, averages 8 pints of blood, and made of up to 60% water. There are 5 vital organs that are essential for survival. The brain, heart, kidneys, liver, and lungs. The human brain is the body's control center, receiving and sending signals to other organs through the nervous system and through secreted hormones.

God's blueprint of the origination of man was that he would live forever. In other words, we were not designed to die. For instance, if you cut your hair or nails they grow back. If you cut yourself, your body creates its own Band-Aid, called a scab, so it can heal. If you break a bone, it will grow back together. The average human body contains approximately 37.2 trillion cells. According to Wikipedia, in an average adult, approximately 50 to 70 billion cells die every day.

These cells are constantly dying but at the same time are regenerating. This means the body is constantly repairing itself.

With all these elements designed by a perfect God working in perfect harmony, I believe it is safe to say that we are made by a perfect design. You are one of those designs.

There are over 7 billion people on this earth. Out of that 7 billion you are the only one like you in existence. There has never been one like you before, there is not one like you now, and there will never be one like you again. You may have a twin, but that twin is not you. You are so special that Mathew 10:30 tells us that the hairs on your head are numbered, not counted, but numbered. If you pull one strand of hair from your head, held it up to God and asked Him what number hair it is, God could tell you it is hair number 1 million, 215 thousand, 322. Do you even know where hair number one is on your head? That's how special you are.

You may have been told you were a mistake or that you were not planned. I'm here to tell you that God planned for you to be here. Your life has a purpose on this earth. Before there was a what, a where, or a when, God stepped out on nothing and called you by your name. After calling out your name, He says I want you to be born for a certain time, a certain place, for a certain reason. You might not know what your purpose is yet because it may not be time for it to be revealed to you.

All the things you've been through or going through were used as a catalyst to prepare you for your purpose. When it's time, it will be revealed to you. You are a single note in the musical composition scored by God Himself. It doesn't matter how you got here. You may have been conceived under the bleachers of a ball game or in the back seat of a SUV. However you got here, God ordained it for you to be here and He loves and adores you.

God made you the way He wanted you to be. So, don't get upset when someone makes fun of your visual aspect. You may feel you have an imperfect look, walk, or even speech, but God made you the way He wanted so He can get the glory out of your life. In the event you are getting bullied, body shamed, or just plain made fun of, just remember they are not ridiculing you, the **creation**, but they are ridiculing God, the **creator**. Okay... back to the first man.

With all its wonder, the human body, or as named in the Bible, the flesh, was only a house that was fully furnished and self-sustaining with a brain. With all those components, this house still needed a denizen to operate and navigate it's use and purpose. To consummate this newly formed relationship between this creation and Himself, God performed a most insinuated action...he blew.

Chapter 2: *The Spirit*

"MYSELF"

Distinct Identity

Myself or My-self is an entity of who we are as a result of our past experiences. The development of our personalities is pretty much based on the good and bad experiences that have occurred in our lives. For instance, you may have a fear of a certain thing. It may have started when something mildly or fully traumatic happened and caused a scary memory. Now your emotions come into play trying to avoid similar events in the future.

The word spirit here in the Greek is derived from the root word pneo (*pneh'-o*), which means to breathe hard or blow.

The spirit, which means breath, is the second component of man. When God blew in man's nostrils, He literally blew a part of Himself into this human foundation. I can imagine God kneeling by this lifeless being and performing spiritual CPR. This gave man life. For this subprogram to be successful, there are two key factors that must be conjoined. There must be an exhaling, which is the giving of life, and an inhaling, which is the receiving of life.

God breathes life into us, so we can exhale worship to Him. When God exhales His glory, we inhale His essence. For example, plants and humans need each other to survive. Humans inhale oxygen from plants and plants survive from the carbon monoxide we exhale.

The breath of God is the life of man. The holy life of man, which is the worship of man, is the joy of God, and the joy of God is our strength. We flourish off the creator and the creator thrives off us. Wow!

Another word for inhale is to also inspire. When we inhale God's spirit, He inspires us to make dreams reality, to make what seems to be impossible...possible. He inspires us to think beyond normal thoughts of human nature. He helps cultivate the faith mechanism in our spiritual anatomy. When He impregnates us with these dreams and visons, He is obligated to provide us with the provisions.

God wants us to lean on and trust in Him, which is why when you were conceived in the womb, He did with you the same as He did with Adam... He blew a part of Himself in you. Why did He do this? He situated a part of His spirit in your being, so He could communicate with Himself in you. Let me explain.

When you were born, the spirit of God was already in you but He was dormant and was waiting to be activated. For example, when you receive a credit card in the mail, it is inactive or dormant. No matter the credit limit, whether it be two hundred or two million dollars, that card is of no use until it is activated. The card company gives a phone number you can dial to place the card into ready mode. After doing so, it can then be used to make purchases.

It is the same way with God's spirit. He is dormant in us until we activate Him. How do we do this? Romans 10:9 tells us, *"That if you confess with your mouth the Lord Jesus and believe in your heart that God raised him from the dead, thou shalt be saved."* When you do this, you are dialing the spiritual digits to activate the spirit of God, so He can then communicate with Himself in you. Now His spirit is affixed with your spirit, or the real you. Not your flesh.

When you see yourself in the mirror, you are not looking at the actual you. You are looking at the house you live in which is your body. The real you is your spirit man living in that body. Because you have actuated the God in you, you now have become an enemy of Satan himself.

The purpose of the enemy is to extract the life or the spirit of God out of you. He does this by creating havocs, distractions, or even small inconveniences in your life, so he can cause a detachment between your spirit and God's.

If you are placed in an air tight room, there is a limited amount of oxygen in it. Eventually, that oxygen you were breathing in will dissipate and is replaced with the carbon monoxide you breathe out and suffocation will ensue. The result would be death. The spirit of God is the oxygen, your trouble is the carbon monoxide, and your life is the room. When you replace your faith (spirit of God) with your worries (doubt), you suffocate, then you spiritually die.

You must understand when you become saved your flesh does not become saved, but your spirit man does. Your spirit evolves but your flesh doesn't. Have you ever been in prayer, or thinking on or doing Godly things and out of nowhere, a crazy non-Godly thought goes through your mind? Well it's not because you are not saved, it's because your flesh still wants to do what it does because of its sinful nature. You have to understand that this body still has the residue of its old ways and habits you did before accepting salvation. That's why this earthly body won't be able to enter the kingdom. We are going to be blessed with a glorified body. A body that was designed like Adam before the fall and sin.

Since your spirit man has changed, the ungodly things you use to do now bothers you. An anguish infiltrates your serenity. It seems as if what some call a gut feeling or intuition, encamps your mentation and makes you to ponder the decision more aggressively to do or not do. Well, there is a reason for that. Something called the spirit of God, the Holy Ghost, or the breath of God, speaks to your spirit man and tries to persuade you to make the right decision by troubling your thought pattern. Why is this? It's because you activated the God in you.

Being able to inhale is a gift of God... Being able to exhale is a mind to live. Thank God for giving us a life worth living.

Chapter 3: *The Soul*

"I"

Self-consciousness; the ego

The "I" part of you is your intelligence or reasoning. It is what looks through your eyes, listens through your ears, and feels through your skin. The "I" part of you is your full consciousness. It processes the information gathered through your senses, so a conclusion can be dictated.

In Genesis 2:7, God breathes into the body and it becomes a living soul. Soul here in the Hebrew is Nephesh (*naw-fash*) which means breathing creature.

The soul is the third and final component of man, and it is also the most critical. When God blew His spirit into the body, it became a living soul or a conscience being. See the soul is our conciseness, judgment, and emotions. It is the result of the body being ignited by God's spirit.

Let me try to explain it this way. We are like a light bulb. When you flip the light switch on, it sends electricity to the bulb. When this happens light comes forth. It is the same way with man. The bulb symbolizes the body, the electricity is the spirit of God, and the light is our soul. When God blew into the body, light or the soul came forth.

Just as the brain is the natural command center of the body, the soul is for the spiritual man. It is our soul that sits between the flesh and the spirit.

Galatians 5:17 tells us how the flesh lusteth against the Spirit, and the Spirit against the flesh. Lusteth here means the sin nature of the body fights against the peace of the spirit and the spirit just can't fellowship with the sin nature of the flesh.

The word lust in the Greek is epithumia (*ep-ee-thoo-mee'-ah*) which means a longing... especially for the forbidden.

This is what you would call an inner conflict between your spirit man and your natural man. This isn't always a bad situation. It's like an internal system of checks and balances. Your flesh will always want to do fleshly things, but it's the strength of our spirit man that will help you prevail.

The spirit and the flesh need to be in conflict because it keeps our soul, or our conscience, mindful that we need to keep our relationship with God strengthened to overcome this spiritual warfare. The flesh is already at an advantage when we are born because we're born with a sin nature. The flesh is already characterized to enact carnal desires from birth. Once we awaken the God in us, we then have accessed power to place under arrest these desires and subdue the flesh for the will of God. How are they strengthened?

Our natural body needs food, water, and nourishments to survive. To strengthen this body, we need both cardiovascular and weight training exercise. In weight training, muscles break down and after resting they build back together stronger, allowing them to meet the demand of what you want them to do. Giving your body the sleep it needs and feeding it the proper foods, can determine the quality of life you will have. These same principles apply to our spiritual man and our flesh.

Going places we shouldn't go, watching things we shouldn't watch, or associating ourselves with people we shouldn't be associated with, are just a few examples of how we feed our flesh.

Remember, the word flesh isn't just about the natural body but in essence it's about human nature.

The nature of sin integrated our spiritual DNA in the garden when Adam, not Eve, ate of the forbidden fruit. When we conduct these carnal activities, we strengthen that DNA and it evolves over time. It dictates our character, attitude and outlook on life itself. In summation, it mandates our mind in how we think.

Just as the spirit is housed in the body, I believe the soul is in the brain. In the front of the brain is the frontal lobe. The frontal lobe is where your judgement and decision-making skills are processed. The soul has to make decisions as to which side to listen to, the spirit or flesh.

The flesh is connected to the carnal world and the spirit is connected to God. Let's say someone makes you mad and a cuss word comes to your mind to say to that person. Now your soul is placed in a position to make the decision as to which one to listen to. Do you listen to your spirit and walk away, or do you listen to your flesh and say some words that are not in the Sunday school book? As I mentioned before, the one that is the strongest will prevail. The job of Satan is to create havoc in your mind (soul), so he can disconnect your spirit from God, allowing it to manifest through the flesh. The result is that cuss word

26

comes out. Your soul is constantly processing whether to follow right or wrong.

Man has not always known good and evil. Before the fall in the garden man only knew the righteousness of God. He was instructed not to eat of the tree of the knowledge of good and evil. The tree in itself wasn't good nor evil, but it contained the knowledge of what was good and what was evil. Just as He gave man the free will to do or not do as He instructed in the garden, He gives us the free will to choose right or wrong today.

Let's be honest, when you were of a carnal life it felt good to the flesh to do wrong. It was rewarding to get away with it and pleasurable to participate in. But when you became Christ like, your spirit felt torment because of your wrong choice. That's because of the God in you. Thank God for his grace! It is God's grace that allows our soul (thoughts, emotions) to be at peace.

1 John 1:5 says: *"If we confess our sins, he is faithful and just to forgive us our sins, and to cleanse us from all unrighteousness"*. When you admitt to God what you have done, accept responsibility, and sincerely seek forgiveness, He has promised He will forgive you. The enemy tries to convince you that you are not worth forgiving or even saving. This is totally a lie. God's love for you is not predicated on your right or wrong actions. There is nothing you can do to make God love you less than He loves you now.

Parents have a child. They love that child first and foremost because he/she is their child. Created by them and an extension of them. That child may break their hearts, let them down, or disappoint them. Even if they must let go, they still love that child.

We are the same in God's sight but to another dimension. We are created by God for God. We are an extension of His glory. The love that He has for us is so much beyond our comprehension. His love is so great that He gave the most important part of who He is, and that is His word wrapped in flesh. Even though we rejected Him before, He still made the provision of giving Himself, so we can have the opportunity to accept Him, become redeemed, and have the right to that same tree of life.

God started this act in the garden. In Genesis 3:22-24, God saw that man had become like Him, Jesus, and the Holy Ghost. Man knew good and evil. You see there was another tree in the garden and that was the tree of life. He said that if they got to the tree of life they would live forever. So, God drove them out of the garden. It wasn't because they sinned that they were driven out, it was because He didn't want them to get to the tree of life. If they would have done so, they would have lived forever with a sin nature and then we wouldn't have a right to that tree. In other words, God was protecting us, so we could have that right and be redeemed back to Him. The only way that would happen would be to give His own life for His creation. What a love!

We might be a wretch undone, we may be a sinner, and we are also taught that we are not worthy. In our own eyes that may be the case, but God thinks differently. He thinks and feels we are worthy, or He would not have given His all for us.

Being a children of God, when we mess up we find ourselves in a guilt complex or conviction. This is where God's grace comes into place. You have to remind yourself that you are the righteousness of God. Satan puts in your mind that God doesn't love you or hates you because you failed. So, you find yourself meditating in your mind what you did wrong and believing God won't forgive you and now you're not forgiving yourself.

If you are not able to let go of the failures of your past, then don't expect to be able to grasp the victories of your future.

Chapter 4: *IT'S THE THOUGHT THAT COUNTS*

Have you ever had someone try to do something special for you, but the end result was not that great? You convinced yourself that even though this isn't my style or my color or done to my liking, etc., you conclude the matter by saying, "It's the thought that counts." Or maybe you did something stupid and someone would ask, "What were you thinking?" Well, it is your thoughts or your way of thinking Satan wants to manipulate.

It is your mind that the enemy uses as a playing field to execute his strategies in your life.

The enemy needs to control your mind (soul), which is the main department of your being, so he can use you as a physical tool to fulfill the task he wants to accomplish in the earth. It all starts with a single thought. His only weapon is placing his thoughts in your mind. He uses what 1John 2:16 says are the lust of the flesh. *"For all that is in the world, the lust of the flesh, and the lust of the eyes, and pride of life, is not of the Father, but is of the world".*

Throughout time man has been and will be enticed by these different areas of temptation. On the natural side, in the brain there is a chemical produced called dopamine, which is mainly known to be the feel-good chemical. It is this powerful chemical that cultivates our sinful pleasures and sinister desires. It is a companion to attention, motivation, and addiction. The fulfillment of lustful cravings, whether it's having a strong desire for attention, or the deep need to smoke a cigarette, overeat, drink alcohol or use drugs, creates a bond with that urge because you actually establish a relationship with the thought of experiencing that dopamine driven fulfillment of pleasure.

You must understand it is not the drug a drug addict is totally addicted to, but he is also addicted to the thought of the pleasure he receives after he uses the drug. So, the addict creates a type of romantic love with the feeling that leaves him wanting more, and the only way to get that feeling is to use the drug again.

According to a team of scientists led by Dr. Helen Fisher at Rutgers, romantic love can be broken down into three categories: lust, attraction, and attachment. I believe I can safely surmise that the enemy takes our thought, places in our mind a great desire (lust), which creates a stimulation of interest (attraction), then ultimately makes a positive feeling of liking (attachment).

James 1:15 tells us, *"Then when lust hath conceived, it bringeth forth sin: and sin, when it is finished, bringeth forth death.".* We already discussed how lust is a passionate corrupted desire or craving. But the word conceived in this verse really started my thought processes turning. To conceive means to form. In the Greek it also means union. For there to be a conception, there has to be a union. A union is the act of uniting two or more things. Just as a man and woman unite to have relations, the woman conceives or becomes pregnant and the result of the conception is a baby. When the baby becomes an adult that child becomes a productive citizen in society.

The first part of this union is lust and the second part is a single thought. Yes, a thought. A thought is an idea or a notion. Believe it or not, Satan is sifting your thoughts to see which ones he can connect with and contaminate. For instance, when a man sees a woman and innocently admires how she looks and then moves on, all is well. But if he sees her and entertains his admiration of her looks, then Satan can take that thought and turn that admiration into a desire. When he ponders on that desire, Satan then attaches to that desire, corrupts it, and turns it into lust. When that thought and lust join each other, lust gets pregnant and has a baby. The baby of this union is sin. Sin grows up and ultimately causes you to miss the mark or God, which is death.

Ghandi quoted something that Satan knows is true.

"Your beliefs become your thoughts,

Your thoughts become your words,

Your words become your actions,

Your actions become your habits,

Your habits become your values."

Satan knows if he can contaminate your beliefs, he can contaminate your thoughts, your words, your actions, your habits, your values, and then ultimately character.

He is constantly trying to replace your thoughts with his. He wants you to think you are addicted. He wants you think no one loves you. He wants you to think you are a failure, so you can fail. **It's not who you are that causes you to fail, it's who you think you are not.** He wants you to think your life is falling apart, but God wants you to know that your life is falling into place. In fact, when you think you have reached rock bottom it's time to rejoice, because now there is only one direction to go....and that's up!!!

Man may give you a penny for your thought, but God gave you His life for your heart.

CHAPTER 5: *CAN'T TOUCH THIS*

An article published in 2005 by The National Science Foundation concerning human thoughts, revealed the average person has between 12,000 to 60,000 thoughts per day. Of those, 80% are negative and 95% are exactly the same repetitive thoughts as the day before. The quality of how we live is heavily based on our thoughts. Our bodies react to how we think, feel, and act. For instance, when we feel guilt or stress, our bodies try to tell us that something is not right. You find yourself having high blood pressure, ulcers, and migraines, among other things. This is what the Devil wants. He wants you to worry. Worrying causes a rift between man and God. So, is worrying a sin? Well, the Bible does not explicitly say it is, but there are scriptures that can bring to conclusion it is.

Psalms 55:22 says, *"Cast thy burden upon the Lord, and he shall sustain thee: he shall never suffer the righteous to be moved."*

In Mathew 6:25, Jesus pleads to them in his Sermon on the Mount to just trust God to take care of them.

1Peter 5:7-8 says, *"Casting all your care upon him, for he careth for you. Be sober, be vigilant; because your adversary the devil, as a roaring lion, walketh about, seeking whom he may devour."* In other words, worrying opens the door for Satan to come in and disrupt our lives.

When we worry, it indicates doubt. Doubt indicates lack of trust. Lack of trust means lack of faith in God. Hebrews 11:6 says, *"But without faith it is impossible to please him: for he that cometh to God must believe that he is, and that he is a rewarder of them that diligently seek him."*

It is safe to surmise that worrying brings sin. What sin? Fear. Why? To sin means to miss the mark God has set for us. This means that worrying is not living up to God's standard. Let us not get worrying confused with being concerned. Worrying is when you torment yourself with or suffer from disturbing thoughts. To be concerned is when a matter engages a person's attention, interest, or care. Worrying opens the door to the spirit of fear

and God does not give us a spirit of fear. Satan and
his demons are constantly surveying our thoughts
to see which ones they can attach their influence
on, even if you are living to your spiritual utmost.

A prime example of an attack on a righteous
man is a very familiar person we know in the Bible.
His name is Job. Yes Job. The man the Bible says
was perfect and upright, feared God, one that
eschewed evil, and there was none like him in the
earth. The man God Himself recommended to
Satan to test. God had confidence in Job not
because he was without fault, because he wasn't.
He was far from perfect in the way we think.
Perfect here meant he was mature in his
relationship with God and eschewed means he
hated evil. When God gave Satan permission to do
what he wanted to Job's possessions and later his
body, Satan looked for a weak point Job would have
so he could attack and drive Job to curse God.
After surveilling Job, he found a point of attack.

The story starts with how Job's sons would
take turns hosting parties in their houses. When
the party was over Job would get up early the next
day and would sacrifice a burnt offering for each
one of his seven sons and three daughters. He did
this because he thought they may have sinned and
cursed God in their hearts. Satan saw this routine
and realized he found Job's weak point. His concern
for his children. He was fearful for his children. It
would be this love and his concern for his children's
souls that Satan would use after weakening him

first by destroying his possessions in a devastating chain of events.

Satan tried to attach to Job's concern, impregnate it with his thoughts, and bare a baby of sin called worrying and fear, which is distrusting God. When that baby of distrust would grow up, Job would miss the mark of God. Satan started by trying to wear Job down using a series of attacks against what he materially possessed. After his servants came to him back to back reporting these tragedies, I can only imagine his strength and focus were staggering, let alone his spiritual mainframe was about to crash. But when he thought it was so close to the end, one more servant entered and tells him what Satan just knew would be the final blow for the knockout. He tells him all his children were dead.

Job is knocked down, severely weakened by this last punch. "All my babies?" he asked. His most cherished and important creations of himself. He sought and entrusted a God to protect them. He stood in the gap for them, presented sacrifices of burnt offerings, and had faith that God would safeguard the hearts of his heart. His babies.

Satan sees Job is down. He just knows he has him out for the count and he won't trust God anymore. When Job was knocked down, his soul, which is his mind, was placed in a position to either follow his flesh or his spirit. His flesh wanted him to stay down, lose faith and reject God. His spirit

38

man wants him to get up, remember who God is, and trust in him. The one that is stronger will prevail.

Satan now tells himself, "Surely he is about to curse his God to his face. My plan is working" ... So he thinks. But because Job was so mature, or perfect, in his relationship with God, it actually backfired on Satan. Verse 20 tells us that Job got up, tore his robe, shaved his head, and then fell down to worship. Wait...What? He worshipped? Yes!!!

Job's spirit man was stronger than his flesh. His soul followed his spirit which is synced with God. Satan couldn't corrupt his thoughts. See Satan may have been allowed to touch his possessions and then his body but one thing he couldn't touch...and that was his mind or his soul. As the saying goes, "THE DEVIL IS DEFEATED"!!!

This shows you don't have to yield to Satan's shenanigans. Even when you feel all is lost or that God has forsaken you. God knows you and knows how much you can handle. So, whenever you are going through, just remember you were built for it. Sometimes we go through not so God can prove Himself to you, but to show you that you trust and believe in Him more than you think.

Psalms 30:5 tells us, *"Weeping may endure for a night, but joy comes in the morning."*

Since joy is coming in the morning, then in order for you to get there, God has no choice but to help you make it through the night.

So, guard your thoughts and let God guard your heart. Remember, Satan may be allowed to touch your possessions and even your body but when it comes to your soul just tell him…**DEVIL, YOU CAN'T TOUCH THIS!!!**

CHAPTER 6: *LUST OF THE FLESH*

We know that lust is a strong desire or craving, but it's not limited to sexual tendencies. The foundation of this definition is the word desire. A desire is to wish or long for something. But I need to emphasis that having desires in itself is not wrong. What we tend to do is confuse lust with desires and the truth of the matter is that humans have natural desires.

When Adam and Eve fell in the garden, mankind's nature became contaminated with sin. Even though this occurred, God has placed in our DNA the ability to think and feel emotions. He has given us desires, imaginations, and most of all the freedom to make choices. In the natural our bodies have desires. When we are hungry we desire food. When we are lonely we desire companionship. When we thirst, we desire water. When we are bound we desire freedom. When there is a sale at the mall, some desire to purchase. (Laughing out loud, sorry Doris). To have a desire for something is not a sin. In fact, Psalms 37:4 says, *"Delight thyself also in the Lord; and he shall give thee the desires of thine heart."* God wants to grant us the desires of our hearts so long as we delight ourselves in him and not the lust of our flesh.

The strongest enemy we have is not Satan or sin, but it is our flesh. Circumstances of life can be very challenging. They can wear us down, but at least we can retreat, regroup and come back for another battle. But the battle of the flesh is an inner battle that is constantly engaged. Sometimes wearing us down to a weakened state and we succumb to its bidding.

Lust of the flesh is an evil desire, almost impossible to beat. It makes sure you will do what it wants you to do. The thing is though, when you conduct the action of a lustful desire, you find yourself not achieving the fulfillment you thought you would. Lust of the flesh is one you don't want to try to fight toe to toe. It doesn't fight fair and it plans to kill.

This lust is a desire for physical gratification through a sinful act. It is doing something to make the flesh feel good. Sex, drugs, food, fighting, among other things, are some of the lusts of the flesh. Paul names the lust of the flesh in Galatians 5:19,

"Now the works of the flesh are manifest, which are these;

Adultery-   voluntary sexual intercourse between a married person and someone other than his or her lawful spouse.

Fornication-   voluntary sexual intercourse between two unmarried people, or two people not married to each other

Uncleanness-   morally impure

Lasciviousness- inclined to lustfulness, lewd, lack of self-control

Idolatry-   excessive or blind adoration

Witchcraft-   magical influence: practices of a witch

Hatred-   extreme hostility

Variance-   controversial

Emulations- jealousy

Wrath-   fits of anger

Strife-   bitter conflict

Seditions-   rebellion

Heresies-   belief or theory that is strongly at odds with established beliefs

Envyings-   covetousness

Murders-   kill someone unlawfully and with premeditation

Drunkenness- intoxicated

Revellings-   riotous behavior

And such like: of the which I tell you before, as I have also told you in time past, that they which do such things shall not inherit the kingdom of God."

As I said before, when we accept Christ as our savior, it is our spirit man that gets saved, not our flesh. Because of this, our flesh and spirit are in constant confliction. Our flesh will always have its corrupted desires because of the downfall of man. The only way we will become free of this is when we exchange it for our glorified body.

Even though we are in a constant fight between our spirit and our flesh, I am so grateful that God is the referee. He knows how to make the right calls.

CHAPTER 7: *LUST OF THE EYE*

William Shakespeare quoted, "The Eyes are the window to the soul". Lust of the eye is a lust that is a temptation to look at things we shouldn't look at or things we shouldn't have. In other words, it is when we look at something or someone with a desire or passion, even when God told us not to. When this occurs, a portal is created that can allow the spirit of coveting to come in, which is a sin. One of the commandments God gave the children of Israel was "thou shalt not covet".

Covet is to have an uncontrolled or wrongful desire for something or someone that belongs to someone else. For example, "I don't see how they have such a beautiful home, I want that house for myself." Or "She has a wonderful husband, I want him." Looking at pornography, wanting what others have, how they look, or their social status are other types of lust of the eye. You want it because it appeals to you. This is generally fueled by the fact that it's not yours or you can't have it.

A good example of lust of the eye is 2 Samuel 11:2. The Bible tells us how one evening David got out of bed and walked on the roof of his house. He saw Bathsheba bathing and she was so beautiful to look at. In this incident, David admired her beauty but looked too long. His eye of admiration became a lust of the eye. This allowed lust to come in and attach itself to his admiration. Lust became pregnant and birth sin. Its name was covet.

We don't need to get lusting after and admiration of confused. To see what someone has and admire it is not wrong. To admire is to look at with wonder, pleasure, or approval. To covet is to wish for it in a wrong way without regard to anybody else.

In order to overcome coveting of the eyes there has to be a covenant with the eyes. A covenant is a formal agreement or pact. Job said in Job 31:1, *"I made a covenant with mine eyes, why then should I think upon a maid?"* In other words, he was saying he made an agreement with his eyes not to lustfully look at a young woman.

Job was upright and a man of integrity. Integrity is to be faithful to moral and ethical principles. His strong belief in following the principles of God were of deep root. He also knew that God sees everything we do and knows everything we think. In Job 31:4 Job gives the reason he wouldn't look at women in a lustful way. *"Doth not he see my ways, and count all my steps?" He was saying isn't God looking at what we do and watching our every move?* Well yes, He is.

Job decided to live his life the way God wanted. We can't hide our sins from God. Living in an age of abundant access to pornography and adulterated sexual expressions, it is important that we guard our eyes. Our eyes are the gate keepers to our mind, which is where we develop our thoughts. When we safe guard our eyes we protect the pathway to our mind. Job committed to not look at women in a lustful way, and it is worth following his example.

I'M NOT TELLING YOU IT'S GONNA BE EASY, BUT I'M TELLING YOU IT'S GONNA BE WORTH IT.

CHAPTER 8: *PRIDE OF LIFE*

Pride of life is a sinful temptation to have greatness or power. The sin of pride is the one sin God hates the most. Pride is trusting in your own strength, righteousness, and wisdom. It is the main thing that caused Satan to fall. He was full of beauty and wisdom, but he had need to be one of greatness. His ego became so engorged with pride that he decided he not only wanted to be like God, but he wanted to be God. *"I will ascend above the heights of the clouds. I will be like the most High"* (Isaiah 14:14).

His spirit of pride caused him to fall from the grace of God. In Isaiah 14:12, he was called the "Son of the Morning", which indicates he was God's first creation. His name was Lucifer, which means holder of light. Because of pride his name was changed to Satan, meaning adversary and was cast out of heaven. Jesus said, *"I beheld Satan as lightning fall from heaven."* Luke 10:18

Well, just what is a spirit of pride? This pride is having an uncontrollable self-esteem. Having an unreasonable opinion of one's own dignity, importance, merit, or superiority. This is not the same as being proud of. Being proud is feeling self-respect or pleasure in something by which you measure your self-worth. When you graduated you were proud of yourself for accomplishing that task. It was a milestone achievement. When your child makes a good grade in school, you are proud of your child and his/her achievement. You can take pride in your accomplishments or your work. There is nothing wrong with that.

To have a spirit of pride is to have a heart of thinking you are better than or believe you are above others. There are some symptoms of a prideful heart.

Allen Parr listed 15 signs of pride in his blog "Pride, 15 Subtle Signs of Pride in Your Life". I thought they would be helpful in using it as a personal assessment of having pride of the heart.

1. ASSUMING YOU ALREADY KNOW SOMETHING WHEN SOMEONE IS TEACHING- When you immediately tune someone out who starts teaching you

something that you may be somewhat familiar with

2. SEEING YOURSELF AS TOO GOOD TO PERFORM CERTAIN TASKS- When someone asks you to do something and your immediate thought is "I of all people shouldn't have to do that. That's for somebody else."

3. BEING TOO PROUD TO ASK FOR HELP - The unwillingness to recognize our own short comings and need for help.

4. FEELING THE NEED TO CONSISTENTLY TEACH PEOPLE THINGS- When someone dominates a conversation because he/she knows something they know most other people don't know much about.

5. TALKING ABOUT YOURSELF A LOT- When you talk a lot about your accomplishments, your education, title, position, and/or financial status.

6. THINKING YOU ARE BETTER THAN OTHERS WHO ARE DIFFERENT OR LESS FORTUNATE- A person can be humble and caring on the outside but in their minds they secretly think they are better than other people who may have different backgrounds, cultures or experience than they do.

7. WHEN YOU DISREGARD THE ADVICE OF OTHERS- Thinking you have all the answers and don't need or see the value in other people's perspectives. You believe you can be successful and reach your goals without advice from others.

8. WHEN YOU ARE CONSISTENTLY CRITICAL- When we tend to put others down because we have a need to feel better about ourselves.

9. CONSISTENT NEED FOR ATTENTION AND AFFIRMATION- When someone constantly needs to be the center of attention and consistent affirmation for their accomplishments, looks, personality, serving, intelligence, and/or physique

10. UNABLE TO RECEIVE CONSTRUCTIVE CRITICISM- When a person struggles to allow other people to speak into their lives and give helpful feedback.

11. OVERLY OBSESSED WITH THEIR PHYSICAL APPEARANCE- When a person is constantly obsessed with how they look and they flaunt their figure or physique in front of others hoping people will notice and gawk at them.

12. UNWILLING TO SUBMIT TO AUTHORITY- When a person is unwilling to submit to authority at work, church, at home or in any other relationship

13. IGNORING PEOPLE'S ATTEMPT TO COMMUNICATE WITH YOU- To blow off people who text or email you because you feel they are not important enough to have any of your time.

14. JUSTIFYING OUR SIN INSTEAD OF ADMITTING IT- When someone graciously points out a sin issue in your life and you get defensive and try to justify it.

15. NAME-DROPPING- When you consistently associate yourself with people who have a prominent position and publicly drop it in conversations hoping people will think you are just as important.

Pride is a sneaky predator that attacks the heart and the victim isn't aware that it has taken position. Pride is a spirit that kills. It will keep you from knowing and recognizing you need God and His grace. Pride is at the bottom of our fear and fear uncovers our lack of trust in God. It makes us become self-reliant and we are not designed to be self-reliant. It is a trap that the righteous and the strong fall into.

There are times when God places you in a position where we have to totally depend on Him. That's how He tests your faith. It's not always that He wants to prove Himself to you, but to expose that you trust Him more than you think. Other times He wants to see if you have enough prayers and faith in you to wait on the result.

You might be tired of praying, but your breakthrough is closer than you think. Can you muster up just one more prayer?

CHAPTER 9: *I CAN'T HEAR YOU, I'M BLIND*

One day my wife was talking to our son telling him to do something he really didn't want to do. He playfully said to her, "I can't hear you, I'm blind". It initially tickled me but then I saw a revelation. This actually happens to us in many ways. For instance, we can't hear true facts about a situation because we are blinded by anger. Or we can't hear warnings of friends that we are being used by someone unfaithful in a relationship because we are blinded by infatuation or love. Through deceits, distractions, and even our logic, Satan at times does us the same way.

In Genesis chapter 3, Satan used a conduit this chapter described to be more subtil than any beast God created...the serpant. The word subtil here in the Hebrew means cunning or clever. Satan knew if he could somehow bring to flourishing the lust of the flesh, the lust of the eye, and the pride of life, it would mean the demise of man's relationship with God as it was.

God had given the instructions directly to Adam, which held him fully accountable for the result of what would be the most catastrophic downfall of man from grace and the beginning of a perpetual task of bringing creator and creation back to its first reality.

Satan knew he couldn't attack Adam directly because his relationship with God was solidified. So, he used his craftiness to reach him through what was close to his heart... Eve. Yes, Eve. His wife, the bone of his bone, flesh of his flesh, and co-executor of all God made. Just as man was the heart of God, Eve was the heart of Adam. Satan knew he could use Eve as a tool of persuasion to bring Adam to a state of reckoning.

Ironically, Satan begins his diabolical plot at the tree of the knowledge of good and evil. It is at this tree Satan used all three temptations with Eve. *"And when the woman saw that the tree was good for food, and that it was pleasant to the eyes, and a tree to be desired to make one wise. She took of the fruit thereof and did eat."* Gen. 3:6.

"The woman saw the tree was good for food"

This is the lust of the flesh. The desire for food is a natural desire of the body. But in this instance, Satan used the body's natural desire as an avenue to become curious about the taste of a food that was forbidden. As an individual, Satan investigates your life to find what interest you. It can be a person, place, or thing that he will strategically place in your path in the hope you will stop and wonder.

"And it was pleasant to the eyes"

This is the lust of the eyes. Once he gets your curiosity going, his next step is to get you to not just look but to gaze. That lingering stare waters the seed of admiration of something good and grows it into a plant of sinful lust for the prohibited. He turns your spiritual eyes from God and locks your natural eyes on the ungodly.

"A tree to be desired to make one wise"

This is the pride of life. We are all tempted to be more than what we are, whether it be physical, financial, or in social status. We tend not to be satisfied in being how God made us. Satan uses this door of lack of confidence to make a room of vanity.

"And gave also unto her husband with her; and he did eat"

Satan succeeded in getting Eve to succumb to his pursuit. He also knew that nothing would happen when Eve ate of the fruit, because Adam was the one held accountable. He subdued Eve and used her to persuade Adam that the fruit was good for food and nothing would happened if he ate of it. He yields to her request and eats of the fruit. Thus, the downfall of mankind. This had to break God's heart.

When we are hurt by someone we truly love, it can cause lasting and sometimes devastating damage. I can only imagine how God feels when we break his heart and he loves us more than we love ourselves.

CHAPTER 10: *DON'T TOUCH THAT TREE*

"And out of the ground made the Lord God to grow every tree that is pleasant to the sight, and good for food; the tree of life also in the midst of the garden, and the tree of knowledge of good and evil." (Genesis 2:9)

In this passage, I noticed some things that are worth bringing out. I never really analyzed this verse before now because I didn't see any relevance to any of the Bible studies I taught or the messages I've preached. It may be because it was written in such a passive way between the verses before and after it. It never ceases to surprise me how viable every word of God is in the Bible. Some of it is unnoticed, even after being read numerous times, but God has a tendency to bring that same hidden treasure to the forefront at the right time.

Oh, by the way, you might feel overlooked or of none importance. You may feel passive between your past and your future. Just remember you are a hidden treasure God is keeping in a viable state until He brings you to the forefront to fulfill the purpose you were created for.

Ok, back to the program.

The first thing I noticed was that God grew every tree to be pleasant to look at and good for food. There were a lot of trees in that garden. God made each tree to be perfect in beauty for man's eyes so he would have no need to look elsewhere. He also made it perfect in taste and nourishment for his body so he wouldn't want to pursue a curious taste or need to seek strength from any other source. He created man with the intention that he would willingly resist sin and choose Him.

TREE OF LIFE

The first named tree mentioned that wasn't given much emphasis and only subtly mentioned once again just before man was cast from the garden was the Tree of Life. We don't place a lot of emphasis on this tree when we talk about the garden, but it played a vital role in the protection of perpetual generations.

The first thing that caught my eye was that this verse made a point to mention, that this tree was in the mist or the middle of the garden. But the point of most interest here is that God didn't tell Adam he couldn't eat of the tree of life. He had free reign to eat of every tree but the one we will discuss later. I believe it is safe to surmise that they were eating of this tree the whole time. This tree symbolized life. Eating of this tree showed a free willed continual trust in God, being covered with His glory, and obedience to the creator. It meant that whatever God said was enough and the relationship between God and man was of profound stability.

THE TREE OF KNOWING

The second named tree, also in the middle of the garden, was the tree of the knowledge of good and evil. This was the only tree and source of food that Adam was commanded not to eat. This tree has gained notoriety over time, mainly because it was the center piece of the table where man's first meal of deceit, lies, temptation, betrayal and death was served. This tree in itself was harmless and probably not even noticed until it was pointed out to be forbidden. Left alone, this tree harmed no one. It wasn't even seeking any attention. But attention was brought to it. First by God commanding not to eat of it, then by Satan tempting Eve to eat of it.

God made it plain to Adam that the day he ate of this tree he would surely die. (Gen. 2:17) But how could this tree bring death if they were still living after eating of it. Before the fall, Adam and Eve didn't know what was good or evil. Obtaining this knowledge wasn't so much about gaining information, but it was about making choices or using judgment.

The knowledge of being able to make choices meant being able to choose between obeying God or submitting to the fallacies of the flesh. They could choose the wisdom of God or judge for themselves what was good and what was evil. Having this knowledge meant they would be like gods. They would no longer be as children having good and evil dictated to them, but they would be as adults making their own determinations of what is good or evil.

The sad thing is, wanting to be like gods wasn't a bad affair but obtaining this knowledge by way of disobedience was the downfall. They could have gotten it the right way, through submission to God. *"Teach me good judgment and knowledge for I have believed thy commandments."* (Ps. 119:66)

STUCK IN THE MIDDLE

These two trees had several things in common. They were unique from the other trees, were pleasant to look at, both good for food, and both were placed in the middle of the garden. The differences they had was as far as the east is from the west. One gave life and the other gave death. One represented submission, the other rebellion. But they both offered options to choose.

In this garden is the symbolism of man's free will to choose Satan's secret plans of deception, and exhibition of God's unconditional love. The trees here grew from the ground of the garden. The garden is an environment developed by God. We are all grown from the ground of the environment we were born in. Our personalities, our logic, and even the way we see ourselves is greatly influenced by the environment we came from. You may have come from a bad environment such as one of abuse, addiction, or even poverty, just to name a few. Just because you were brought up in that atmosphere, it doesn't mean you have to stay in it. We are stuck in the middle of making decisions that give us life or decisions that lead to death.

Every tree was pleasant to look at

God has placed all of us on the earth as trees. We are pleasant to the eyes of those in the world that look at us when we live a life of holiness and exemplify a spirit of worship. *"O worship the Lord in the beauty of holiness: fear before him, all the earth."* Ps. 96:9

Every tree was good for food

If we allow ourselves to be beautiful to the eyes of those that don't know God, we can create a desire or hunger for them to want God. In order to satisfy that hunger we must become a source of food. That food is the word of God. If we don't store our spiritual pantries with God's word, we can't feed anyone.

Both trees were in the middle

God has always allowed man the obscure gift of freewill. When Eve was at the tree talking to Satan, I realized Eve was debating with him the issue of it being right or wrong to eat of the tree. See Eve didn't know what was good or evil but she did know what was right and wrong. She knew it was right to eat of the other trees and it was wrong to eat of the tree in question. The freedom of a man's will to choose is always put to the test of choosing what is right and what is wrong but it wasn't until after the fall man knew good and evil. What do I mean?

To be good is to be morally excellent, virtuous, and righteous.

To be right is to be in accordance with what is good, proper or just.

To be evil is to be morally wrong or bad; immoral, wicked.

To be wrong is to not be in accordance with what is morally right or good.

Having morals is being concerned with the principle or rules of right conduct.

Let me see if I can sum this up. To be good is to **be** what is right, to be right is to **do** what is good. To be evil is to **be** what is wrong, and to be wrong is to **do** what is evil. We are always stuck between these two trees. Our soul is constantly trying to decide to be right or do wrong.

If you have chosen to be right, then DON'T TOUCH THAT TREE, because if you touch it, you're going to taste it, and if you taste it, you're going to believe it, and if you believe it, you're going to follow it.

CHAPTER 11: *YOUR WORDS ARE ALIVE*

Every invention, medical breakthrough, architectural wonder, song, and even every word we speak is started with a single thought.

We express our thoughts in various ways. The main way we express what we feel is through words. Words reveal the thoughts of one person to another whether they are verbal or written. This book you are reading started with my thoughts that were inspired by the Holy Ghost. I expressed these thoughts through a series of typed words. I had them replicated to be shared through print for those who are interested and could read what I feel after much prayer, studying, and research.

These words you are reading also give you who don't know me personally, a view of how I think and what I believe. If you ever want to know how someone thinks, just listen to their words in a conversation.

It is amazing how sometimes what we really feel can be misrepresented by the wrong choice of words. So, we often use the term "that's not what I meant." There are also times we say things out of emotions and meant what was said but didn't mean to say it. So, the next statement made is, "Excuse me, I didn't mean to say that." To excuse someone is to forgive and to be excused is to be forgiven.

Well I'm so glad God always says what He means. He knows He loves us. He used His best words of compassion, Jesus the word of God, to express it. He used His personal stationary, the cross, to display it. To solidify the fact that He meant it, He ends the letter with "it is finished." I thank God for making it so clear that He loves us in spite of. He really does have a way with words.

With that being the case, the words you speak are an expression of what you have in your heart, which is your mind or your soul. The words you choose to express how you feel or what you are thinking are very important in the spiritual realm. *"Life and death are in the power of the tongue."* Proverbs 18:21. Your words can bless you or they can destroy you.

To think you are worthless is one thing but to speak you are worthless is another. See God and Satan are waiting for you to speak into the atmosphere. There are times friends jokingly say to me, "You the man...you have all the money." I would jokingly reply with "Nah doc, I'm broke, I'm just trying to make it". Then we would just chuckle and go on with other subjects. In time it occurred to me that I was actually cursing myself. I was speaking into the atmosphere that I was broke which meant I would never have money. So, I went in prayer and started rebuking every curse I placed on myself with my words even when I was a kid. Now when someone speaks that over me I say I receive it. If it's something negative I rebuke it. See God uses the positive you speak into your life for your good but Satan uses the negative things you speak in your life against you. So, when you do or say something outside the will or principles of God, just remember, "Excuse me God, I didn't need to say that".

Say what you feel, but be careful what you speak, especially if they are based off heightened emotions...because someone is listening

CHAPTER 12: *GOD GAVE HIS WORD*

There was a time when a man's word was his bond.   When two people made an agreement all it took was a handshake and that sealed the deal. Now we are in a time where parents and children, sister and brother, best friends, even fellow church members have to sign a legal document to hold each other accountable. Our courts are now being bombarded with family members and friends suing each other over simple agendas.

The most important thing you have is your word, which is an expression of your character. For instance, when you go on an interview, the interviewer has already assessed you in the first thirty seconds based on your outward appearance and actions. But then there has to be an evaluation of who you are inside. Your words give them an inner view of who you are through a series of answers to questions and comments you make. The words you speak carry an arsenal of importance.

Words can encourage or dishearten, build up or tear down, set free or place in bondage. I think you get the idea. Our words not only have power in the natural but very much so in the spirit realm as well. To receive the full effect of how important and powerful your words are, we must first understand how important God's words are.

John 1:1 says *"In the beginning was the Word, and the Word was with God, and the Word was God."* God Himself started everything He created with a single thought. When He spoke the words, let there be, His words went forth and created. He inspired man to write His thoughts and feelings into words in the Old Testament. The problem was those written words could not be touched and they couldn't touch back. They had no emotions or compassion. They were not alive. This is why Jesus is so important. Jesus is the thought of God or the living word of God wrapped in flesh. His word is so important that God said, *"Heaven and earth shall pass away: but my words shall not pass away."* Mathew 24:35.

In John 1:1 it starts with the phrase "in the beginning", which is referring to Genesis 1:1 where it also starts with "in the beginning". The word beginning here in the Hebrew is Bara, which means dateless past. "Was the word" is the thought of God, "was with God" means face to face, and "was God" is God was the word. Verse 3 says "all things were made by him", Him meaning His word, which means His word was the creator not the created.

1 John 5:7 says, *"For there are three that bear record in heaven, the Father, the Word, and the Holy Ghost: and these three are one."* This is the indicator that Jesus is the word of God and has always been. So, if I wrote a summation based on these translations, it would read something like this.

"In the dateless past was the thought of God, God spoke His thought and He and His word (Jesus) were face to face, and His word (Jesus) is God, and through His word (Jesus) He created everything: and nothing was made without Him (Jesus)."

Here we find God used Jesus to create everything. Just as God used His words to create, He has given us the same authority. We have the authority to speak over our circumstances, our health, our families, our lives. In Ephesians 3:20 we see He is able to do exceeding abundantly above all that we **ask** or **think,** according to the power that **works in us.** He knows our thoughts and our desires. He wants to grant them to us but He is waiting on us to do one thing...speak it. Speak it into the atmosphere. Speak it into existence. To do what Romans 4:17 says God does: Call those things which be not as though they were.

God used His words to create. To create is to make something out of nothing. To build is to make something from other materials. For example, God created Adam but He built Eve. He created Adam because He was developed out of nothing.

He built Eve because He used Adam's rib to make her. Like God, we can speak into the atmosphere and create miracles of healings, financial breakthroughs, reconciliations of families, or even companionship.

So, when we read or study the word of God, we are not just spending time with words but we are spending time with God Himself. The Bible gives us an inner view of who God is and how He thinks. When we ingest the words of God in our spirit, we expand the thoughts of God in our soul. So, we not only need to read the word but we need to relate to it.

In Isaiah 55:10-11, God tells us how the rain and snow falls from heaven and doesn't return. But, it waters the earth and causes things to grow so planters can have seeds and the hungry can have bread to eat. Just like that, He said the word that comes out of His mouth won't come back to Him empty handed but it will finish doing what He told it to do.

Don't believe me? Check this out. God sent His word and made it flesh. It dwelt among us and was rejected by His own. His word healed the sick and raised the dead. His word was betrayed, turned over to those that despised Him and was beaten. His word was given a crown of thorns and nailed to a cross. His word took on the sins of the world and redeemed man back to his creator. When the task God's word was sent to do was finished, His word returned to Him and was not empty handed.

What am I saying? **GOD GAVE HIS WORD.**

CHAPTER 13: *OUT OF MIND, OUT OF SIGHT*

Romans 12:2 says, *"And be not conformed to this world: but be ye transformed by the renewing of your mind, that ye may prove what is that good, and acceptable, and perfect, will of God."*

There is a saying that says, "Out of sight, Out of mind". This statement means that a person stops thinking about something or someone if he or she does not see that thing or person for a period of time. In this chapter, you will see how Satan's success is based upon applying the opposite.

BE NOT CONFORMED

This world we live in has its own philosophical concepts and its logic is far from the spiritual principals of God. When we make the decision to crucify the old man or our old spirit, we begin the journey of abandoning our old ways of thinking and accepting the will of God.

In this verse, Paul instructs us not to be conformed to this world. To conform is to be similar in attitudes, practices, characters, etc. of a society or group. Sometimes we feel in order to be accepted by a person or group, or what we call a click, we have to act and think like them. To think like the world is to follow the ways of the flesh and the flesh is another word for human nature. As I stated before, human nature was tainted in the garden and now has the tendency to be attracted to the complete opposite of God's biblical principles. In other words, we are born doing wrong.

My wife Doris once asked me, "Does a baby have to be taught to do wrong?" I quickly answered yes. She made it very clear that she disagreed. After about an hour and a half of debating the issue, I felt a need to stop and ask for a more in-depth understanding of her question. I finally realized that she was right.

I used the example, I lay some money on a table and a toddler comes in and innocently takes the money, then goes to another room to play with it. My reasoning was that the child didn't know it was wrong, therefore, the child wasn't wrong. But if I taught the child how to steal the money, then I taught the child to do wrong. She made me understand that whether the child knew it was right or wrong is not the point. It was wrong for the child to take the money and no one had to tell him to do it. Therefore, the baby did wrong on its own. Well, I had no further argument concerning the matter. Then I came to understand that we don't have to teach the child to do wrong, but we do have to teach the child that the act of taking the money without permission was wrong.

When we have the mind of the world, then our thinking is clouded by the logic of the flesh that there is nothing wrong with our actions. Until there is a conviction by the Holy Ghost, we remain in the error of our carnal psychology. That conviction can only be brought to light by the hearing of the word or the thought of God. It is listening to and accepting the thought of God that enlightens us that we are in error and there is a need to change our way of thinking.

Paul tells us in Romans 12:1 to present our bodies a living sacrifice. The Message Bible says it like this, *"Take your everyday, ordinary, life--- your sleeping, eating---going-to-work, and walking-around life---and place it before God as an offering."* When we do this, we don't think or act like those of the world. I often say that just because I live in the world, doesn't mean I have to be of the world. But at the same time, just because you are not of this world, it doesn't mean you have to be ignorant of what's in it.

BE YE TRANSFORMED

Paul goes on to say to be transformed. To transform is to change in condition, nature, or character. In other words, repent. The Greek word for repent is, metanoya. Meta means change, noya means mind, which is where we get the word metamorphosis. Transforming is actually a metamorphosis. Naturally, this is when animals undergo extreme, rapid, physical changes sometime after birth. Metamorphosis is when a larva completely changes its body plan to become an adult. The result can change its entire body design. For those species that use metamorphosis, it is typically required for sexual maturity. If metamorphosis didn't occur, tadpoles could not become frogs or larvae couldn't become full-grown adults, such as butterflies, capable of reproduction. If they don't reproduce, that species dies out.

It is the same way with man. Shortly after we are born into the kingdom, there is an extreme, rapid change or metamorphosis in the way we think. The Holy Ghost completely changes our spiritual body plan to become spiritual adults. Our thoughts match with the thoughts of God causing us to reproduce His biblical principles in the form of witnessing, preaching, and teaching, among other ways. If spiritual transformations don't occur, the sinners can't become saints who become spiritually grown adults capable of reproducing God's word. If we don't reproduce, we will die out and Satan prevails.

RENEWING YOUR MIND

Next, Paul tells us how to be transformed. It is by the renewing of our minds. In the Greek it means to restore, reverse, or renovation. In order for this to occur, we have to let go of worldly conformation, so we can experience internal transformation, and achieve spiritual regeneration. Restoring our minds is an ongoing task because Satan is constantly trying to move in for occupation. It is our minds he wants to control so he can replace the thoughts of God with his thoughts.

It is your mind where the devil chooses to fight you to conquer your emotions, relationships, peace, happiness, health and even finances to name a few. But when God gives you a new mind He gives you new weapons of defense. See when you win the battles of your mind then you reap the benefits of victory through your flesh. You might be in the mist of one of these battles now. But remember, in your life God has already gahead in time and won the war. Since you serve the God of no limits, then that makes you a no limit soldier.

"I will meditate in thy precepts and have respect unto thy ways." Psalms 119:15. Satan knows that when we continue to meditate on the heart of God, we will always see the hand of God. He wants to change what we think about, so he can remove who we think about. He uses distractions to pull us apart from the thought God, so he can create an attraction with the opinion of the flesh. Satan looks for vacancies in our minds and when we are not focused, he is coming in to occupy. If he can keep God out of mind, then God will become out of sight.

THE FACE OF GOD LEAVES YOUR SIGHT WHEN THE THOUGHT OF GOD LEAVES YOUR MIND,

.

CHAPTER 14: *I AM THAT I AM*

"And God said unto Moses, I AM THAT I AM: and he said, Thus shalt thou say unto the children of Israel, I AM hath sent me unto you." Exodus 3:14

When you were born, there was a word spoken over you. As you began to get a since of understanding, you noticed this unit of sound was repeatedly spoken towards you. After much repetition and intellectual growth, you began to realize that this unit of language was used to get your attention and no one else. It was your name.

Just what is a name? According to Wikipedia, A name is a term used for identification. See names can be used to identify animals, groups, or even objects. But right now the name I want to explore is the individual name.

An individual name is a distinguishing word by which someone is personally known by or assigned such as, "Stanley", "Kyria", "Mattie", or "Adrian". It is customary for a person to have a personal name, which is a first and last name. The last name is usually the family name, because it is shared by members of the same family. Middle names are used as another way to identify and at times used for personal reasons.

God has been given many names throughout the Old Testament. We call Him God, but that's not His name. His name in the Hebrew is YHWH. The Hebrew language does not have vowels which is why it's spelled the way it is. Because the English language uses vowels, we spell His name Yahweh. His name was so sacred that they would not even say it.

In our reference verse above, we see that God introduces Himself to Moses through a burning bush that is not being consumed. He shares with Moses how He has heard the cries of His children and that He has come to deliver them. He gives Moses the assignment of being the one to lead them out. Understandably Moses asked this spiritual being who would he say sent him? He would answer with what is the meaning of the word YHWH, "I AM", which is to say, "HE IS" or "TO BE".

"I" (first name)

Using the word "I" is referring to one's self. I is the ego of God, which is how He thinks, feels, or distinguishes Himself from others. This applies to us as well. It is how we react to the outside world.

The difference between God and man is that when man says I, a lot of times, he is consciously or subconsciously comparing himself to someone else, such as, "I can do it better than he can", or it is going along with someone else, such as, "Duan and I shifted the paradigm of the project".

When you go to court as a witness, you have to be sworn in while placing your hand on the Bible and ending the oath with "so help me God". To swear is to make a formal statement or declare something is true by some sacred being or object, such as God or the Bible. Man has to call in a higher entity as a witness to guarantee that he is telling the truth or that he will do what he promised he would do. *"Thou shalt fear the Lord thy God, and serve him, and shalt swear by his name."* Deuteronomy 6:13.

When God refers to Himself, there is none to compare to Himself to. His "I" status stands alone and doesn't have to swear to anyone or thing. He is the most sovereign God. When He swears, He swears to Himself. *"For when God made promise to Abraham, because he could swear by no greater, he sware by himself."* Hebrews 6:13.

God's will and thoughts are far beyond any man or object. Man's finite intellection is of no comparison to God's infinite mentation. *"For my thoughts are not your thoughts, neither are your ways my ways, saith the Lord."* Isaiah 55:8. God is God and He stands alone.

"AM" (middle name)

"AM" is the first person singular of the present tense of be. "Be" is to exist or live. It also means to occupy a place or position and to continue to remain as before. This actually describes God. AM is the time essence of God and He stands outside of time. Let me explain.

God holds the position of supremacy. He is Omniscient, which means He is all knowing. He is aware of the past, present, and future. Nothing takes Him by surprise. He is always the present tense of "BE" or existence. He always has, He always is, and always will exist in the present and will never change. *"Jesus Christ the same yesterday, and today, and forever."* Hebrews 13:8.

God is also Omnipresent, which means He is all present. He exists and lives occupying every place being everywhere at the same time. There is no location where He does not dwell.

"THAT" (last name)

Webster's dictionary tells us that the word "that" is used to identify a specific person or thing observed by the person speaking. Such as, "that's his wife over there". It also is to refer to a specific thing previously mentioned, known, or understood, such as, "That's a good idea".

When God says He is that, He is referring to being specifically what it is you need Him to be. When you need Him to be your healer, then He proclaims I am your healer. You need Him to be your deliverer, then He proclaims, I am your deliverer.

WHAT'S YOUR NAME?

I have tried to explain in a short but informative way, the origin, purpose, and importance of a name. As I said before, God has been called many names but those were descriptions of what He is. I have attempted to explain this by presenting a micro interpretation of who He is by analyzing His name.

When a man and woman become married, it is customary that the woman takes on the family name, which is also called the last name or birth name of the husband. Doing this means the wife replaces her family name with his. She may also choose to make her birth name her maiden name.

Now she inherits a married name, which is a family name espoused by a person when married.

When we become saved, we become a part of the church or the kingdom of God. Jesus is married to the church. The church is the bride of Jesus. Jesus is the son of God, which means His surname is the family name of God. When we became a part of the church, then it means we are married to Christ, who has the family name of God because He is God's son. Whew!! So, when we married Christ, we replaced our family name with His. How? I am so glad you asked!

A NEW NAME

"Verily, verily, I say unto you, He that believeth on me hath everlasting life. **I am that bread** *of life."* John 6:47-48. In these verses we see an example of what I have explained about the "I AM That" of God. "I", is the feelings of God, "AM", is the present timing of God, and "That", is the specific identity of what He can be.

Jesus tells the people in this scripture that their fathers ate manna from heaven and are dead. But there is a bread from heaven that man can eat and he won't die. Jesus saw there was a need and he wanted to let them know that he can be the answer to it. So, he tells them "I am that bread". In other words, he was saying,

85

"I",   my feelings
"AM",   at this present time
"THAT",   is am your living (specific) bread.

Now, let's take this a little further. When we married into the family of God we took on His last name, THAT. But we didn't make it our last name, it became our first name. Because unlike the wife, when she marries she keeps her first name which means she still is identified by who she was before marriage with her first name. But when we take on the name of God, we totally give up our old identity to take the identity of God. We actually lose our first name because our first name was sinner. Now it is Redeemed.

When we take on the name of God, it goes a little like this: He says His name is I AM THAT. Now, when He replaces the word THAT with something specific as Jesus did in the previous verse regarding the living bread, we see this:

God says, "I Am your healer." Now because we take on the last name of God to replace our first name, our response would be, "Healed I AM".

God is I AM THAT and you are THAT I AM.

God's promise	Your response
I am your deliverer	Delivered I am
I am your redeemer	Redeemed I am
I am your comforter	Comforted I am

I think you get the idea.

"THAT", is what we need God to be and "THAT", is what God wants us to be.

It is the THAT of God that will free you. It is the THAT of God that will work miracles in your life, break strongholds, reconcile your families, heal your finances, and place joy back in your soul!!!!

Open your mouth and shout with a victorious voice,

I NEED THAT!!!

CHAPTER 15: *DIVIDED and CONQUERED*

"And if a house be divided against itself, that house cannot stand." Mark 3:24.

I know in this verse when Jesus said house, he was referring to the members of a family. When the members of a household work together and are on one accord, there is strength. But when someone comes in and spreads discord, or as my grand folks would say, throw salt between them, this causes division, and they are going to be destroyed.

To divide is to separate, to separate is to keep apart by an intervening barrier, and a form of intervening is to mediate. Satan uses sin to separate us from God, God uses the blood of His son as an intervening barrier to save us from the penalties of sin, and Jesus stands as the mediator between us and God. *"For there is one God, and one mediator between God and men, the man Christ Jesus;"* 1Timothy 2:5

As I said before, the body is the house where the spirit and the soul abide. Satan is attempting to divide you with intention to conquer. When your flesh is under subjection, it is the result of your spirit and your soul working in harmony. It's because you are walking in the spirit and overcoming the lust or strong desires of your flesh. This makes Satan a little upset. He tries to cast discord between your spirit and your soul. Some of the discord he cast are the cares of life. He creates havoc in our lives so he can destroy our relationship with God.

Our lives are like the structure of a building. A single room structure has four corners that supports a roof. It takes all four corners to stand at the same time in order for the roof to be sustained. How does that apply to us? Let me explain. There are four corners to our lives that sustain us: Our finances, relationships, faith, and health. If Satan can cause one of these corners to falter, then it sets the other corners up to become compromised.

For example, you lose your job. It causes a challenge in your **finances**. This causes problems in the **relationship** with your spouse because it's not recovering like you want and you become stressed. Your stress causes **health** problems like, migraines, ulcers, strokes, etc. now your **faith** in God begins to waver. When this happens, the roof collapses. You can start with either of these and it causes a chain reaction with the others.

Satan is continually surveying the pillars of your life to see which one is weak or has a crack. Cracks in the support beam of a building have to be examined and repaired by an expert, so it can be brought back to a sound structure. This applies to the support beams of our lives.

The pillars of our finances, relationships, health, and faith, when attacked, can become weakened by life's storms and travesties. If not placed on a scheduled maintenance plan, such as prayer, Bible study, attending church, and fasting, the construction of your life can deteriorate and crumble. This allows God to come in to inspect our life's anatomical structure. When He sees there is a crack or potential failure, God comes in with His infinite wisdom and loving hands to fix the damage and shure up our support beams. Then once again, we can stand with confidence as an ambassador for the Kingdom of God.

Sometimes we tend to ignore the maintenance schedule of spending time with God. In this instance, a crack of separation of our soul from our spirit causes our spirit to detach from that of God. We begin to try fixing it on our own strength. We try to figure it out trusting in our own comprehensions. The problem with this is that we are not designed to be strong. We are not made to carry those burdens. We are designed to trust and depend on God to carry our burdens. *"Trust in the Lord with all thine heart; and lean not unto thine own understanding."* Proverbs 3:5.

ALL JACKED UP

I was riding down the highway on my way to an event. I noticed the sky started developing a formation of storm clouds with lightning, but it wasn't raining. About that time, I had a flat. Traffic was heavy and the shoulder of the road I pulled over on was slanted. I got my equipment out to change the tire. I became very apprehensive because of the lightning, the cars speeding by, and the slant on the road shoulder.

I was like, God, you see this traffic, the lightning, and all this metal around me right? Seriously? But the tire had to be changed. I started jacking up my SUV, then all of a sudden, the truck slid off the jack because of the slanted shoulder. I began to try it again, but the jack was broken from the fall. Now I'm in a bad situation. Out of the corner of my eye I noticed a car coming towards me and of course, I'm hoping it wasn't a stray vehicle. Thank God it wasn't. It was a friend of mine pulling up behind me. What a sight for these sore eyes. He gets out saying, "I was passing by and thought that may have been you. Then when I saw that big ole bald head, I knew it was you. Ha Ha Ray Brown, very funny.

Anyway, I told him my situation with the jack so he goes to get his. Mind you, I have an SUV and he was driving a sedan. So, in my mind I'm thinking this wasn't going to work. But hey, I had no choice. I lifted my vehicle as far as his jack would go, but there was another problem. My spare was a little taller than my other tires, which meant that the jack was just shy of being tall enough to put the spare on to the truck. At this point we were starting to feel a few sprinkles and we didn't know what to do.

We started looking in the ditch and alongside the road for limbs or anything we thought could be used to place on top of the jack so we could get a little more height. We didn't find anything. Then a thought occurred to me. I had a duffle bag of hard back Bibles in my vehicle that I kept for people to use when I preached or conducted Bible studies at different places. I yelled out, "Hey doc, I found something!" "What you got?" he asked. I held one of the Bibles up and I said, "I got the word!" I let the vehicle down, placed one of the Bibles on the ground and put the jack on top of it. I jacked it up to the max and low and behold it was just right to put the spare on. What's my point? Wow y'all, again with the questions. Ok, here's the revelation I received when I pulled off to finish my journey.

Oh, before I forget... Hey Ray, thanks for the help doc! Now, here's the revelation.

God showed me something in the spirit. The truck represented my burden, the spare was my prayer, the jack was me, and the Bible represents itself, the Word. The jack by itself could only lift the truck to a certain point and that wasn't enough to lift it high enough to put the spare on the truck. But when I placed it on the word, it reached the height I needed.

When we try to lift our burdens with our own strength, we can only go so far. Like I said before, we are not designed to lift or carry burdens. We wear ourselves down trying to lift and carry. The tire was bigger than my normal circumstances and was beyond my capabilities.

But when we stand on the word! Wait don't run shouting yet, let me finish. Ha ha... God wants you to stand on His word. The word that says you are the first and not the last, above only and not beneath, a lender and not a borrower, He will give you the desires of your heart, He is the God that healeth thee, and He will never leave you nor forsake you! Yep, that word! See using your own strength and understanding, will only take you so high. But when you stand on His word, He will give you the strength and the height to stand high enough to see the answer to your prayer being placed on your spiritual SUV, "STANDING UNDER VICTORY". That just came to me while I

93

was typing this sentence. Glory! When people ask how you doing, how you smiling in your storm, how you making it through those lies and rumors? Just tell them I'm riding in my SUV, I'm Standing Under Victory!

So, jack up your disappointments, jack up your debts, and jack up your failures. So, how's my situation? **IT'S ALL JACKED UP!**

KEEP IT TOGETHER

Jesus was asked the question by the Pharisees, if it was lawful for a man to put away his wife. At the conclusion of his response he said, *"What therefore God hath joined together, let not man put asunder."* Mark 10:9. He also stated that if a man put away his wife and married another, he committed adultery.

Adultery is voluntary sexual intercourse between a married person and someone other than his or her lawful spouse. There are more types of intercourse than just sexual. These are the physical aspects of adultery and intercourse, but there is a spiritual side to this as well.

When we accept Christ in our lives, we become married to him. Just as the man and woman become one flesh, with Christ we become one spirit. The man and woman are no longer two but become one, so it is that Christ and man become one. No longer does the husband or wife belong to themselves but are subject to each other. When married to Christ, we no longer belong to our individual selves but to each other.

Satan wants to separate us from Christ. He tries to lure us into having spiritual intercourse with the world. Remember, one meaning of intercourse is the interchange of thoughts and feelings. He tries to get us to rationalize the thoughts of the world so that we start to agree with them. Our thoughts become compromised and we find ourselves agreeing with and sleeping with the enemy, committing adultery against Christ.

Satan takes what God put together and puts it asunder. See it was God that put the body and the spirit together which birth the soul. All being one but having different functions. To be asunder is to be apart or widely separate. This started in the mind with a thought that was entertained, took root and sprouted. We start separating our spirit from God's and give the flesh strength over our spirit, allowing the soul to choose to succumb to the stronger. The end result...Divided and Conquered.

When a marriage is in trouble, there has to be a fight to keep it together. You may argue, words may get twisted creating havoc and confusion, but there must be a fight for it to survive. There has to be a fight to keep your spirit, soul, and flesh together. Your spirit and your flesh may argue, your mind may get confused, but you have to remember that God is not the author of confusion.

The word confuse comes from the Latin meaning to mix or mingle together. As God develops us into what he **needs** us to be, the enemy tries to mingle or mix it with what we **want** to be. Hence becoming confused by the author of confusion.

There has to be a **defusing** of our will so that we can **fuse** to God's will. If God's light is not on in you, then you may want to check your spiritual breaker... because you may have a blown fuse.

IM NOT TELLING YOU IT'S GONNA BE EASY, BUT I'M TELLING YOU IT'S GONNA BE WORTH IT...

CHAPTER 16: *YOU ARE NOT ALONE*

"And the Lord God said, it is not good that the man should be alone; I will make him an help meet for him." Genesis 2:18.

Adam was by himself in the garden until God saw it wasn't good for him to be alone. Alone means to be "all one". God made man just like Himself, self-contained, which is how it is the woman came out of the man. But that's another book.

God knew Adam not only needed someone to help him, but to also love him, comfort him, encourage him, remind him, and okay, stroke his ego. You know, make him feel like he can do anything.

God made the relationship of husband and wife a mirror image of the marriage between Christ and the church. So, He made Adam what the Bible calls an Help Meet. In the Hebrew, **help** means **aide** and **meet** means **suitable**. So, God made Adam an aide suitable for him. The enemy wants you to think you are alone.

When God saw us in the spirit realm He knew it was not good for our spirit man to be alone. So, He gave us an aide suitable for us. That aide is the Holy Ghost, the breath of the great "I AM". The Holy Ghost plays a vital role in our lives. He loves us, John 3:16. He encourages us, he comforts, teaches, and reminds us. John 14:26. And yes, strokes our ego, making us believe we can do anything.

He dwells within us being a friend closer than a brother. He listens to our most private thoughts, understands our deepest fears, and hand delivers our prayers to God. He is our advocate, our defender.

One way he defends us is by convicting us. God uses the gift of conviction to impress us with a sense of guilt when we fall short of His mark. When He sees a part of our character is not lined with His principles and recognizes we are struggling in that area, through the Holy Ghost, He lets us know He is there to help us out of it.

There are some daily things you can do that will help you maintain this relationship and help you cope with life's daily challenges.

When you begin to execute the following applications, just remember it won't be easy and will take practice. You may get off track but just get back on. I beg to differ with the saying that practice makes perfect because it doesn't.

Perfect practice makes perfect. You can actually practice something wrong.

1. DON'T WORRY

"Rejoice the soul of thy servant: for unto thee, O Lord, do I lift up my soul." Psalm 86:4.

Worrying is tormenting yourself with or to suffer from disturbing thoughts. Negative thoughts activate your brain's right pre-fontal cortex, which sits next to your stress center. When your brain releases stress hormones, like adrenaline, it does a number on your immune system and causes health problems.

We were not designed to worry. But when we do, our body reacts to the meditation of our negative thoughts. When these thoughts resonate in our mind or soul, we become a disturbed or unsettled being. Jesus told the disciples to not let their hearts be troubled when he told them he was about to leave. Remember, I told you the word let is a word of permission. In other words, he was telling them not to permit the peace of their souls or the thoughts of their minds be disturbed.

Just like the spirit is in the body, my belief is that your soul or mind is in the front of the brain, where the frontal lobe is also. Have you ever been troubled in your mind and you laid your head on the lap of someone, and when they rubbed your head it soothed you? Or when you get your hair washed and while they were rubbing the shampoo into your scalp do you became relaxed and dose off? Did a kiss on the forehead give you a feeling of comfort or reassurance? Or even more importantly, when someone laid hands on your forehead to pray for you, did you feel a sense of peacde? Well that's because these actions were soothing your soul.

If your soul is weary, wounded, scorned, or just plain empty, God wants to restore it. To restore is to bring back to a state of health, soundness, or vigor. *"He restoreth my soul: he leadeth me in the paths of righteousness for his name's sake."* Psalm 23:3.

God created you with storms in mind. So, when your life's storms are raging, don't be afraid. You see the only thing that will be blown away is your mind when you see how God brings you out.

2. KEEP YOUR JOY

"A cheerful heart is good medicine, but a crushed spirit dries up the bones." Proverbs 17:22 (NIV)

The one thing God wants for us, is to be happy. He wants us to enjoy life to its fullest. He wants us to have joy, which means having a state of happiness. Your joy is blossomed from your peace. Peace is a freedom of mind from annoyance, distraction, anxiety, an obsession, etc. If you recall, these are some of the things I stated the Devil uses to take our peace. He wants your peace so he can take your joy. The Devil uses storms in an effort to pull you down and out.

Tornadoes and hurricanes create havoc and destruction. But in the middle of these storms is the eye where there is peace. If God doesn't take you out of the storm, ask Him to put you in the middle of it, because that's where He is. He is that peace in the middle of your storm. You may lose a lot of things but don't lose your peace. This is Satan's way of stealing your happiness.

When there is no happiness there is no joy, when there's no joy there is no peace, when there is no peace there is no hope, when there's no hope there's no life, when there's no life there's only death.

"These things have I spoken unto you, that my joy might remain in you, and that your joy might be full." John 15:11.

But if you happen to lose that joy, Philippians 4:4 says *"Rejoice in the Lord always; again I say, rejoice."* To rejoice is to be glad or have joy again. You can only have joy again if you go through sad or disappointing times. So, go ahead and shed your tears, moan through your pains, and hurt through your burdens. You might feel a little weak right now, but remember if God is in you, your joy is coming again. The joy and re-joy of the Lord is your strength.

3. LAUGH

"A cheerful heart brings a smile to your face; a sad heart makes it hard to get through the day." Proverbs 15:13 (MSG bible)

A smile is to assume a facial expression indicating pleasure, favor, or amusement. Studies have shown a single smile can trigger a flood of endorphins in your brain compatible to eating hundreds of chocolate bars or being handed a fistful of cash. Seeing someone else smile also causes you to smile to. People who smile a lot tend to be healthier, more successful, and looked at as being more competent.

The one thing I have realized about God is that He has a sense of humor. I shared this thought with Doris one day and she replies, "I know he does. He made you, didn't He?"

Laughter is a gift that God has placed in our human behavior. It is closely tied to joy because the feeling of joy can promote laughter. Even Scientist tell us that laughter, humor, and joy are an important part of life. It's part of the universal human language. With all the thousands of languages and dialects in the world, laughter seems to be the one we all can understand.

Babies are a good example of how laughter is in our nature. They can laugh before they can even talk. Even those that are born blind or deaf, still have the capability to laugh. It has been proven that laughter increases blood flow in the body and leads to reductions in stress hormones. When we laugh, our brain releases endorphins, which is the body's natural feel good chemical. Endorphins also promote an overall sense of well-being and can even relieve pain. It increases the circulation of antibodies in the blood stream and makes us more resistant to infections. This is God's prescription of the body's self-producing healing medicine.

Laughter can even alleviate tense situations. For instance, when there is a room of escalated emotions, somebody doing or saying something funny can sometimes relieve anxiety and calm everyone down enough to be able talk more sensibly and reach a peaceful resolution. Laughter is a medicine to your body, spirit, and soul.

Laughter is a gift that is contagious. Have you ever been a little down and walked into a room full of laughter and not even knowing what was funny, began laughing yourself? Use this gift to not only help you but those around you as well.

4. PRAY

To pray is to offer devout petition, praise, and thanks to God. Prayer is your quality time with him. This is the time you can pour every feeling, confess every violation, request your heart's desires, and most importantly give thanks and show gratitude. This is the time you can be completely honest and transparent. This is the time to forgive and ask for forgiveness. But most importantly, prayer is about developing your relationship with God. You may not always see certain prayers answered, at least the way you want, but it doesn't mean prayer doesn't work. **It often times seems like God is the slowest man to be on time.**

5. PRAISE AND WORSHIP

Anyone can praise God. In fact, God gives any and everyone permission to praise him. *"Let everything that hath breath praise the Lord. Praise ye the Lord."* Psalm 150:6. To praise is the act of expressing approval or admiration. We praise God for what He has done.

But when it comes to worship, there has to be a relationship with Him. See, we worship God because of who He is. There has to be a connection of your spirit with God's. Which means not everyone can worship Him. Worship is to show adoring reverence, which is an expression of the feeling or attitude of deep respect. *"God is a spirit: and they that worship him must worship him in spirit and in truth."* John 4:24.

GIVE HIM YOUR PRAISE AND YOUR WORSHIP.

Your praise (thanking God for what He's done) will get you to the gate...but your worship (loving Him for who He is) will get you to the throne.

CHAPTER 17: *YOU ARE WHAT YOU THINK*

"For as he thinketh in his heart so is he:" Proverbs 23:7

As I was growing up, my father said to me on several occasions, "Son, I know you are old enough to do what you want. But if you never listen to anything else I tell you, remember this. Before you ever do or say anything, just stop... and think." I have applied this to my life and have given those same words of wisdom to my son.

To think is to use your mind rationally and objectively in evaluating or dealing with a given situation. Thinking is also having a belief or opinion. These are the corner stones to help us conclude what we will choose to do or say.

It's hard to control what random thoughts visit or travel through the atmosphere of your mind. However, you do have control on whether they linger or take root in the soil of your mental estate.

When you allow negative thoughts to infiltrate and occupy your mind, you put yourself at risk of making decisions that will delay or even abort the destiny of your life. The enemy will do this in such a subtle way that you won't even notice the changes in you until it's too late.

DO YOU SEE WHAT I SEE?

"Just as water mirrors your face, so your face mirrors your heart." Proverbs 27:19 MSG

Solomon talks about how water can be like a mirror that reflects or gives back an image of what is in front of it. The image he refers to here is the face of a man. Mirrors reveal to us things other people physically see of us. This can be good and sometimes not so pleasant. Especially when it's something unpleasant others see but don't tell you. Such as something in or on your teeth when you smile or something in your nose. The good thing is that once it is revealed to you in the mirror you can correct it. This is the same with our character. I can imagine God asking the question, "Do you see what I see?"

There are mirrors that reflect our hearts. People can be a reflection of you. For instance, children can be a reflection of their parents, students the reflection of their teacher, members of a church can be the reflection of their pastor, organizations can be the reflection of their leaders, etc.

One mirror of most significance that reflects who we are or who we are not is the word of God. It helps us examine our thoughts, intentions, and emotions. Sometimes we are blinded by lust, envy, or strife and it keeps us from seeing the truth about ourselves. Again, God asks the question, "Do you see what I see?"

"Examine me, O Lord, and prove me; try my reins and my heart." Psalms 26:2.

The heart of a man is the center of his total personality, emotions, feelings, or even his intuition. In other words, it is how he thinks. The face of a man is his reputation, dignity, or prestige, which is how he acts. Your actions are a reflection of how you think. The way you think is exemplified by your reactions to what happens to you in life.

Our lives are composed of a series of events that were predestined to occur before time was created. Since God stands outside of time, He has already created the path of our lives and has gone to the end of it establishing the journey we will need to follow in order to fulfill the destiny and purpose of our existence.

Your DNA was grafted with certain gifts and talents because you were designed with purpose. Along with those gifts and talents God also allows you to use the gift of free will to use it how you desire.

The way you use that free will is determined by the heart of your thoughts, which is your character. Your character is the total things that you do, feel, and think. These traits are used to judge if you are good or bad, strong or weak. This is how your reputation is established.

God has entrusted you with a gift with the belief you will be the steward its needs to properly nurture it. He knows that our character has flaws and there is a risk that it can be used, not for His glory, but for the carnal appetite of the world. Doing this is an abuse of that gift. Abuse is abnormal use of something. For instance, you can have a gift of persuasion, but instead of using it to compel souls to the kingdom, you use it to swindle people out of money.

The bad choices we make sometimes will cause us to get off the course God has created for us to follow. When this happens, God creates circumstances that gets us back on track through His grace. It is only by His grace and mercy that we are able to get back in His vision. His grace is receiving benefits we don't deserve, and His Mercy is not receiving punishments we do deserve.

Proverbs 18:16 tells us that a man's gift makes room for him and it will get the attention of famous people. Whether we are born with it or it's developed, we develop our character along with our flaws. No matter how talented or gifted we may be, our character flaws can hinder or stop us from reaching the destination God has planned for our lives.

Don't let your gift take you where your character cannot keep you.

WHO YA WITH?

"Iron sharpeneth iron; so a man sharpeneth the countenance of his friend." Proverbs 27:17. KJV

The old technique of using an iron hammer to form the edge of a heated piece of iron was common knowledge. If one of the pieces were heated to a high enough temperature, it would become pliable and could be sharpened by the other. This made it capable of being formed into a tool or weapon. The process of an iron hammer against softer, heated iron is more than likely the generator of this passage of scripture.

It means we need to work with one another to improve our strengths and subdue each other's weaknesses. We do this by holding ourselves accountable to someone we can trust.

"Confess your faults one to another, and pray one for another, that ye may be healed. The effectual fervent prayer of a righteous man availeth much." James 5:16

Confessing our faults pulls the covers off our weaknesses or strongholds that debilitates and retards our spiritual growth in God. The challenge at times is finding someone we can confess our faults to.

When we are fighting hidden failures, the enemy uses this to hold us hostage and blackmails us with the attempt to imprison us to a corner of darkness and shame. But if we can confess to another piece of iron that is harder and is able to sharpen us in our time of vulnerability and frailty, the enemy can't demand the ransom of our body, spirit, or soul.

If you want to know how you think, look at the five closest people you hang with. Are they people that you can depend on to help you stay strong in the faith or are they ones that allow or even encourage you to compromise your beliefs and biblical principles? So, who are you with?

When you lower your standards to hang with people who have no standards, then you are just hanging

CHAPTER 18: *A CLOSED MOUTH DON'T GET FED*

"Ask and it shall be given you, seek and ye shall find, knock, ant it shall be opened unto you."
Mathew 7:7.

I think it is safe to assume that you have heard the saying, "A closed mouth don't get fed". It means if you don't ask for what you want, don't expect to get it. When you go to a drive through and they ask to take your order, you can't expect them to make it with extra pickles because you thought it. You have to open your mouth and tell them.

In a relationship, you may wonder why you don't get out of it what you need or want. It most likely could be because you haven't said what it is you require. You can't always assume the other person knows what you need, like, or dislike. Even babies, that cannot talk, communicates in some form that there is a problem or conveys some sort of motion or gesture indicating what they want or don't want.

We as children of God, have the ability to speak what we desire from Him. God wants to give us the desires of our heart but He wants us to ask.

In the previous verse, Jesus tells the crowd how they can obtain what they want from God.

ASK

To ask here is to request or petition that something be given to you or done for you. The time we usually make our request to God is during our prayer time. The problem is when our prayer time is hindered, dwindled, or even diminished, our request becomes undocumented because there isn't a record of seeking God for the result needed in certain areas of our lives.

Asking is also a way of seeking permission. The way you ask can display a form of humility. When I was in high school and needed to go to the rest room, I would ask the teacher, "Ms. Jones, can I go to the bathroom?" Now days it's more of a statement with a taste of entitlement instead of permission. The student will say, "Ms. Jones, you'll let me go to the bathroom?" This generation or even you may not see the difference in the two statements but there is one. God wants us to come to Him with humility.

SEEK

Isaiah 55:6 tells us to seek the Lord while He may be found. To seek is to search or look for. God wants us to look for Him which is to yearn for Him.

As a child, my friends and I would play a game called Hide and Seek. I would close my eyes and place my head in the fold of my arm and count to one hundred by fives. While counting, my friends would run and hide somewhere they thought they could not be found. When I counted to one hundred, I would yell out, "Ready or not, here I come." I would start looking for them while they were hoping I wouldn't find them so they could run back to the base and be safe.

God is so the opposite of that. There are times He seems to be out of touch. It might even seem like you can't feel Him. Like your prayers are just bouncing off the walls and falling on deaf ears. But I'm here to tell you that He is there. He is hiding. He is creating a desire to seek him, not because He doesn't want to be found, but quite the opposite. He hides because He wants to be sought after and most importantly....to find Him. We seek Him by fasting, prayer, and reading His word.

Believe me, if you truly seek Him, you will find Him. He is waiting to hear, "Ready or not...here I come".

When you work all week or month, you look for your paycheck because you have met the requirements to receive it. When you make your request known to God and have the faith believing what you prayed for will happen, start looking for it to come to flourishing because you met the requirements to make it come to pass.

KNOCK

To knock is to strike with a sounding blow with the fist or anything hard, especially on a door or window. In this case, it means to take actions.

When you have made your request and you are looking for it to happen, now it's time to do the work. If you asked God for a job, and you are looking for it to happen because you believe, then you have to start doing the work to make it happen. You must fill out applications and go on interviews.

You have to knock on the doors of opportunity and the windows of hope. Since knocking is making a pounding noise, then let the noise be a sound of praise and thanksgiving for what He is about to do. This knocks down the door or disappointments and opens the windows of blessing. Let your inner trumpet blow a sound of rejoicing just like the children of Israel did with the walls of Jericho. Those walls must come down. Satan wants to keep your mouth closed so you won't pray to ask. If you don't ask, God has nothing to work with to give to you.

When you don't receive anything, you won't have anything to praise Him for and celebrate. Therefore, your closed mouth won't get fed.

MY POINT

As I studied this verse, I noticed something very interesting about his passage. The three things Jesus said to do was to **Ask** (make your request), **Seek** (look for it to happen), and **Knock** (go get it). Take the first letter of each word:

A sk

S eek

K nock

When you put those letters together, you get the word...**ASK!!** God is so deep!! That's right, He simply wants you to ask.

The reason you may not have the answer to your prayer maybe because you told Him what you wanted with a slight attitude instead of asking with humility.

CONCLUSION OF THE MATTER

"I press toward the mark for the high prize of the high calling of God in Christ Jesus." Philippians 3:14

To press is to move or push something by weight or force in a certain direction or into a certain position. The only time for a need to push or press is when there is an obstruction or blockage of a path. That obstruction can be a person or thing.

The mark is heaven. The main purpose of our desire to live this life is to be with God in Heaven. Man is beginning to feel less of an urgency to reach this mark because we are making where we are now our heaven. Technology has made life so convenient and we are so blessed in so many ways that we are developing a lack of luster for God's heaven. We must not let this steal or obstruct or desire to push for the mark of Heaven.

The calling of God is a high calling. This call comes from Heaven which is where the prize of eternal life is giving for heeding to and executing the call God has place on your life.

God has placed this call in Christ Jesus. The only way to get to Heaven is through Christ Jesus, who is the word of God. It is through this word that He calls us. The only way to acknowledge the call is by faith which is only obtained by hearing. And what do we need to hear? You got it... the word, which is Jesus.

"So then faith cometh by hearing, and hearing by the word of God." Romans 10:17

Pressing toward the mark of the high calling doesn't mean you won't encounter problems, disappointments, stumble, or even fall completely sometimes, which is why we have to press for it. So, if you find yourself falling short of the mark, it doesn't mean you are out of the calling. No matter what...focus on the call and keep it moving.

God will always be there to pick up the pieces when you are broken, He will always be there to strengthen you when you are weak, protect you when in danger, and most importantly, love you unconditionally.

BROKEN PIECES STILL FIT

I broke an item once and it hurt my feelings because it had sentimental value to me. But because I still had the pieces, I found a good bonding agent, put it back together and gave it time to bond. It became like new.

God is the same way with us. You might have a broken heart, which is crippling, or a broken spirit, which is devastating. God's feelings are hurt that you are broken because you are of sentimental value to Him. The great thing is that God still has the pieces of your life. So, with the bonding agent of His love and allowing time for you to heal, you won't be just like new, but better than new. So, sit back, lay your head in His bosom, and let the healing begin.

On your journey towards fulfilling God's destiny for your life, always remember, at times you may find that you have to stand by yourself, but you are never alone. When they ask who is with you, just tell them...**ME, MYSELF, and I...AM**

Lord I'm not so perfect, but I'm willing

"And the peace of God, which passeth all understanding, shall keep your hearts and minds through Christ Jesus."

Philippians 4:7

Made in the USA
Columbia, SC
30 August 2019